GOD MOMENTS
FOR BUSY PEOPLE

30 reflections to bring peace and rest

Jennifer Rees Larcombe

MONARCH
BOOKS

Published by Monarch Books
an imprint of
Lion Hudson Limited
Wilkinson House, Jordan Hill Business Park,
Banbury Road, Oxford OX2 8DR, England
Email: monarch@lionhudson.com
www.lionhudson.com/monarch

ISBN 978 0 85721 845 2

First edition 2018

Acknowledgments
See page 92

A catalogue record for this book is available from the British Library

Printed and bound in Serbia, February 2018, LH55

To Papa John and Carol,
thank you for all your love and kindness to me.

Contents

Introduction

My life is just so busy these days! Probably yours is too? We don't have long, leisurely hours to spend with God, but we all know that being with Him on a daily basis is vital if we want to move deeper into His heart. So we just have to snatch those odd spaces between jobs as we hurtle through our busy days – and turn them into God Moments. I am convinced that when we deliberately open our ears to Him at the beginning of the day, He uses all the little things we see, hear, and experience as we go through any ordinary day to share with us the secrets of His heart.

Over the past year I have been jotting down the seed ideas of these "God Moments". They so often come to me at awkward times that I have to jot them down quickly or they are gone by the time I reach my computer. So I scribble all over the inside cover of my cheque book, a paper napkin, or even a petrol receipt – providing I can also find a biro!

There is therefore no particular order or theme to this book; it is simply a way of turning odd moments into God Moments! Just keep it by your kettle, leave it in the loo, or pack it into your laptop bag before running out of the door.

May reading it bless you as much as I have been blessed through writing it!

Jennifer Rees Larcombe, Summer 2016

1
Desperate for You

"I'm desperate for You." That phrase pops up often in songs we sing at our church, but what does "desperate" really mean? Because life down here on Planet Earth is often so tough, of course we are desperate for God's help – perhaps for healing, for finance, or to find a spouse. We need a supernatural Dad to protect and provide for us, and He loves it when we run to Him in our desperation. He always answers our prayers, albeit in His time and in His way!

Yet there is another kind of being "desperate" for God, which I believe completely delights His heart. It is when we say, "Lord I'm desperate for *You*, Yourself alone and not what You can do for me; I yearn to know You intimately, to experience Your friendship, and to be aware of Your presence with me every minute of my life." That kind of "desperate" is very rare indeed.

The apostle Paul had always wanted to become a Pharisee, keeping God's rules perfectly. Then one day he met Jesus, which completely changed his life-goal. Realizing all his rule-keeping was as worthless as garbage he wrote, "I want to know

Christ – yes… becoming like him" (Philippians 3:10). That is all he wanted for the rest of his life. He was insatiably hungry for more of Jesus and longed to become His lookalike.

I'm not saying that I have this all together, that I have it made. But I am well on my way, reaching out for Christ, who has so wondrously reached out for me.

Philippians 3:1s2 (MSG)

Lord, I'm mind-blown when I realize You made me for Yourself, to be Your friend and companion. You don't exist just to make my life comfortable, and I don't exist just to serve You. You love me for myself alone and yearn for me to return Your love.

2
God's Priority

While it is great to be "desperate" for the Lord's company, it is even more brain-stretching to realize He is desperate for ours! Crowds of people were always surrounding Jesus, pushing each other aside because they wanted healing, a free lunch, the excitement of seeing a miracle, or to hear some radical statement. He had so much compassion that He loved helping every one of them, but I wonder if He ever felt lonely in the middle of those demanding hoards?

We humans have a built-in longing to be loved, unconditionally, just for ourselves, not for what we can do or give. Because we are made in His image, Jesus would have had the same deep yearning. Just think how much it would have meant to Him when He found someone in those crowds who had come for no other reason than that they loved Him and wanted to be close.

He still loves to help us today, as we pray for all the things we badly need – or think we want. Just occasionally He has the joy of finding one of us who simply wants to give Him pleasure, comfort, or encouragement. When He chose the people who became His greatest servants He chose them first and foremost so they could be His companions. "I no longer call you servants… I have called you friends" (John 15:15).

> Then Jesus went up a hill and called to himself the men he wanted… "I have chosen you to be with me," he told them. "I will also send you to preach…"
>
> Mark 3:13–14 (GNB)

Lord, I know that You are so vast
You fill the entire universe – which
You actually made, and have
been holding together ever since
[Colossians 1:16b–17]. Yet You
want to sit in my kitchen and laugh
with me when I burn the toast – yet
again! What an honour! Thank You!

3
The Outcast

When I was tiny we kept chickens. There was always one who would be excluded by all the rest, and they would often peck it until it was raw and bleeding. I used to get so upset when I saw these unfortunate individuals huddle in the corner of the chicken run, excluded and alone. When I went to school I discovered children do the same to other kids! And later I realized adults do it too!

Treatment like that breaks our heart, but sometimes when the hard outer shells of our hearts are broken by adversity it makes it easier for the love of God to find its way in through the cracks and broken pieces. Perhaps that is why God says He is especially close to the broken-hearted (Psalm 34:18)?

Most of us want to be completely understood by at least one other person – and still loved anyway! So it hurts horribly when that person, who we thought was so close, suddenly seems to be pulling away. Yet it is *in* that kind of pain that we most easily discover how perfectly God understands us – and *still* loves us to the uttermost!

God keeps an eye on his friends,
his ears pick up every moan and groan …
Is anyone crying for help? God is listening,
ready to rescue you. If your heart is broken, you'll find God right there;

if you're kicked in the gut, he'll help you catch your breath.
Disciples so often get into trouble;
still, God is there every time.
He's your bodyguard, shielding every bone;
not even a finger gets broken.

Psalm 34:15, 17–20 (MSG)

Thank You, Lord, that You understand what it feels like to be rejected, misunderstood, and looked down on by other people. I love it that You understand exactly how I feel – and stand with me, even when everyone else seems to be tearing me apart.

4
Intimacy is Possible!

Have you ever thought, "No way! I could never have an intimate relationship with God! I have far too many responsibilities to sit for hours reading the Bible. Perhaps when I retire"? Yet it is possible for any of us, however frenetically busy, to have a continuous love relationship with God. To "pray without ceasing" (1 Thessalonians 5:17, KJV) does not mean muttering words all day; it's just realizing that He is with us, involved and interested in every detail of what we are doing.

When you love someone and they are sitting right next to you, you can communicate without long speeches; you convey what you want to say by a quick glance in their direction. We can do the same with Jesus, using the eyes of faith, however busy we may be. I find it easier to do that if I think of myself turning towards Him, just as if I could see Him there next to me. Perhaps I'll give Him an invisible smile of thanks or raise an enquiring eyebrow when I need to know what He wants me to do or say next. I sense Him laughing with me when something funny happens, and I'm often aware of His compassion when things go wrong.

I don't beat myself up when I lose our connection during hectic patches of the day; I just enjoy the fact that He's still there waiting when life calms down again. Bill Johnson describes this "reconnection" as "turning our affection towards Him". I like that!

The eyes of the Lord are on those... whose hope is in his unfailing love.

God keeps an eye on his friends.

Psalm 34:15 (MSG)

Lord, I love it that, even though I often forget You are there, You still stay beside me all through the day, never taking Your loving eyes off me for a moment. Please help me to become more continuously aware of Your presence beside me – always.

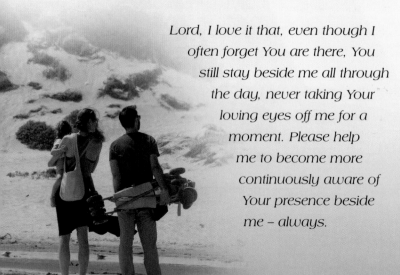

5
Hurt but Not Harmed

The other day I was out walking my favourite footpath; it winds up a steep hill towards a single tree, which dominates the skyline. Out of breath, I went over to lean against its trunk. It was only then that I saw the scar, which I'd never noticed before.

Obviously, when the tree was young, someone must have tried to put up a notice by hammering lots of nails into its bark and consequently damaged the developing trunk. The ugly scar had lengthened and twisted as the tree grew, even though the nails and the notice were long gone. I suddenly realized something: the young tree had survived the damage and trauma and still managed to grow to its full, magnificent height. The wound left by the nails had even added to its beauty.

As a counsellor, I've often heard people say, "I can never make anything of my life because I had such a terrible childhood." Of course we can be damaged in childhood by cruel words, abuse, and rigid control; they leave jagged scars like the nails on that oak tree. Yet I firmly believe that past experiences do not have to stunt our growth or prevent us from reaching our full potential – when we are willing to open ourselves to God's healing. The scars may never fade, but perhaps they stay to remind us of God's totally accepting grace.

> *The righteous... shall grow like a*
> *cedar in Lebanon...*
> *They shall still bear fruit in old age;*
> *They shall be fresh and flourishing,*
> *To declare that the Lord is upright.*
> Psalm 92:12, 14–15 (NKJV)

Lord, I didn't want those things to happen to me when I was a child. They should not have happened! They hurt me badly, but once I'd given You all the pain You began to help me forgive, and then used it all to shape me into who I am. You're amazing!

6
Apologies from a Mother

Last evening I was asked to speak to a men's group. As I was nervously praying about what on earth I could possibly talk about, I felt the Lord wanted me to apologize to them on behalf of their mothers. They looked slightly bewildered when I stood up and did just that, but by the end some were blowing their noses suspiciously often.

The words mothers say to their children can adversely affect the way they think about themselves for the rest of their lives. As a mother, that makes my hair stand on end, because under the pressure of parenting we can say all kinds of things we don't really mean! "You're nothing but trouble!" "I wish you'd been a girl!" "You're so stupid/lazy/difficult!" "Why can't you behave like your big sister?" We don't realize that this kind of constant disapproval can be seriously damaging. "The words of the reckless pierce like swords" (Proverbs 12:18).

As those men looked back at me I could see all kinds of painful memories beginning to surface. So I hurriedly reminded them that forgiving the person who spoke harmful, negative words to us is the way to start undoing the damage they did. The teachers, parents, siblings, or grannies who spoke them over us may never say sorry, but forgiveness does not depend on their acknowledgment of how much they hurt us. We can forgive and find healing even if they happen to be long since dead!

> *And when you stand praying, if you hold anything against anyone, forgive them, so that your Father in heaven may forgive you your sins.*
>
> Mark 11:25

> *Lord, I know the things my teacher said to me have had a devastating effect on my confidence ever since. I've forgiven her, but I guess I won't just do that once; it's a choice I'll need to make many times over!*

7
Acorns and Pine Nuts

I have seven huge oak trees in my garden. They dwarf my bungalow with their massive bulk. I love them in winter when their branches are bare so I can watch squirrels doing their acrobatics; but I also appreciate the fresh green leaves that give us shade for summer picnics in the garden. Right now their acorns are falling with such considerable force that one dented the top of my son-in-law's new sports car. He certainly doesn't like oak trees any more! Have you ever thought how astonishing it is that something as tiny as an acorn can grow into such a gigantic structure?

Raking up acorns always reminds me of the worst weeks of my life. My situation was so bad it looked as if I would lose everything that mattered to me. I did not even feel I had enough faith to pray. So I picked up an acorn and kept it in my pocket for days to remind me that God only needs us to plant a tiny bit of faith in our hearts before He is able to begin growing something massive. As Jesus Himself once said, "God's kingdom is like a pine nut that a farmer plants. It is quite small as seeds go, but

in the course of years it grows into a huge pine tree, and eagles build nests in it" (Matthew 13:31–32, MSG).

The Lord has anointed me to comfort all who mourn…
They will be called oaks of righteousness,
a planting of the Lord,
for the display of his splendour.

Isaiah 61:1, 3

Lord, when I look back at that awful time when I kept the little acorn in my pocket, I just have to marvel at how You have looked after me and sorted out every detail of my life. Thank You! Please let me never take You for granted.

8
Simply Enjoying Him

I love my life at Beauty From Ashes – a little retreat centre in Kent. My days are very full: praying with people, listening, comforting, and making endless cups of tea. At the end of the day I escape into the garden and relax as I water and deadhead in summer or rake up leaves and make bonfires in winter. I need time to process some of the terrible stories I've been told during the day, and hand the people, and their pain, over to the Lord to hold. I can't do that in words; I sense it happens automatically as I focus on the things He has made.

Yesterday, as I was enjoying the colourful patio pots and borders, I felt sad that our visitors haven't been able to sit out here and enjoy the garden much because it seems to have been raining for months. Then I felt the Lord say, "But you and I have enjoyed the garden together. I love being here with you." Something in me just melted.

Of course He wants to be the place where we dump our painful emotions and the first person we go to for help when something goes wrong, but it is so easy to forget that He also loves being with us, silently enjoying whatever we happen to be doing.

Do you have a place where you can keep Him company and be refreshed? It does not have to be an actual location – it could be an imaginary place hidden inside your head or a memory of a time when you felt particularly blessed by Him.

> *"Only in returning to me and*
> *resting in me will you be saved.*
> *In quietness and confidence is your strength."*
> Isaiah 30:15 (NLT)

Thank You, Lord, for not just using me as Your servant but also wanting me as Your friend.

9
Bad News

Nine months ago I went to see an oncology consultant with someone I love very much. The news they gave him was very bad indeed, and as I listened to the prognosis I felt irritated by the words that floated into my head: "Give thanks in all circumstances" (1 Thessalonians 5:18). I know we don't have to thank God for bad things like illness and pain, but in every situation it is usually possible to see God's kindness and grace somewhere. That day in that gloomy hospital department I found myself telling Him, "There is absolutely *nothing* I could possibly force myself to thank You for right now! Too many of us need this man!"

Then I felt that God replied, "If you put all this into My hands, you could thank Me that I am in complete control."

That has often felt hard to believe since, but gradually I've seen a miracle happening in my friend. No, not healing from cancer, but a deep inner healing from so much that has hurt and damaged him in the past. I've been astonished as I've watched the Lord gently peel away layers of self-protection that have been wound tightly around his heart by past pain and adversity. Discovering God as the loving father he never had has radically changed this big, quiet man who never felt quite "good enough". Now, right on the brink of heaven, he is influencing many more people than he ever has before. So now, finally, I really am able to thank the Lord that He is in control!

Always giving thanks to God the Father for everything, in the name of our Lord Jesus Christ.

Ephesians 5:20

Thank You, Lord, that we really can trust You to hold our lives safely in Your hands as You bring good out of even the worst situations.

10
Dustbin Revelations

The other day I was sure the Lord was saying to me, "Try to live in your spirit rather than your soul." I was scrubbing out the dustbins at the time, so I had plenty of opportunity to wonder what He meant. I guess our spirits are where we connect with Him – hear His voice, speak to Him in prayer. Our souls, on the other hand, are the invisible human part of us where we think, feel, and make our own choices. Even when we have given ourselves to the Lord completely, this human part of us still prefers to be in control, rather than letting God be Sovereign. This is why we find ourselves feeling grumpy and selfish or being tempted to do things we know the Lord would not like (Romans 8:5–6).

God knows that rather than being dominated by human thinking, emotions, or desires, we'll be safer and happier if we live above that earthly part of ourselves. Living in the Spirit means aiming to get so close to the Lord that we instinctively know what He thinks about whatever situation we are in, how He feels about it, and what He wants to do with it.

By the time my dustbin was clean, I realized that all God wants is for me to remember that I am "seated with him in heavenly realms in Christ Jesus" (Ephesians 2:6), looking down at my life from His angle.

I no longer live, but Christ lives in me.

Galatians 2:20

"In him we live and move and have our being."

Acts 17:28

Lord, I've often envied the apostles living with You for three years, watching all You did and listening to everything You said. But I guess now, by Your Spirit, we not only live with You, but You live in us and we live in You!

11
Verbal Abuse

I live with a vicious bully who verbally abuses me. He constantly tells me I'm useless, stupid, in the way! A while back I thought he'd gone, but suddenly he's back, determined to get me down. I wouldn't tolerate him in my life if he were human, but he's just a voice in my ear. I guess he is taking advantage of me because I've been struggling lately, feeling slightly disconnected from God. Church and the Bible have felt so boring that I guess I had stopped expecting to hear God's voice any more. All I could hear was condemnation from my Voice.

Yesterday, feeling rather desperate, I cried out to the Lord for rescue. I cannot think why I didn't do that sooner! My morning Bible reading contained His answer, telling me He thinks I'm precious, honoured in His sight, and that He loves me (Isaiah 43:4). So now I have to make a choice: do I listen and believe God's voice, or do I keep on tuning in to hear that other Voice – which sounds suspiciously like a mixture of a teacher in my past and a fearsome aunt!

I told the Voice to get lost in Jesus' name, and to never come and whisper his lies in my ear again. I'm going to listen to words like this instead:

"For I know the plans I have for you," declares the Lord, "plans to prosper you and not to harm you, plans to give you hope and a future."

Jeremiah 29:11

"I have loved you with an everlasting love;
I have drawn you with unfailing kindness."

Jeremiah 31:3

Lord, I'm so sorry I've allowed life to get me down lately, and for letting myself listen to that other voice instead of Yours. Please train my spiritual ears to hear You –
and help me to be more confident that it's Your voice I'm hearing!

12
Barbed Wire

I woke up this morning with a vivid picture in my head. Someone had wrapped themselves in coils of rusty barbed wire. As I got dressed I realized just how many people I've met who are trapped in self-made cages like that. They always feel lonely, even in a crowd, and long for friendship and love – yet they feel compelled to push everyone away.

I guess they are trapped by their fear of rejection. Perhaps they have been hurt so often that they have erected barriers to protect themselves from ever being hurt again. I remember one girl who kept losing her job because she was so bad tempered. If anyone dared to get close to her they were so badly scratched by her "barbed wire" they never tried again.

Not all our barriers look that hostile. Sometimes we keep ourselves safe from rejection and human contact with shyness, computers, a hobby, or even social media. I had a horrid shock when I was training as a counsellor. We were put into small groups and allowed to say anything we liked without inhibitions. Someone turned to me and said, "Your trouble is you've covered yourself with pink candyfloss. It says, 'Don't

hurt me; I'm too nice and sweet.' Actually, you're just fragile."
I fumed silently for days before I realized he was totally right;
dismantling my artificial façade has given me relationships that
are both real and satisfying.

"The Lord does not look at the things people look at. People look at the outward appearance, but the Lord looks at the heart."

1 Samuel 16:7

Lord, Your love for people always made You reach out to them, even if their self-designed barriers hurt You. Please demolish all my self-protective strategies so I can be loved by You, and also love and be loved by others.

13
Untapped Power

I have the power to make something dramatic happen instantly on the far side of the world! I can cause my son-in-law to leap out of bed in a fury – if I forget time zones and ring him during the day, which is actually the middle of his night! I only did that once, and definitely learnt a lesson the hard way! All the same, my great-grandmother would have been awed by my amazing power!

Actually, prayer is even more powerful than a phone: I can affect someone far away just as dynamically by praying for them! We've probably all found ourselves suddenly thinking of someone for no apparent reason and felt the Lord wanted us to pray for them. That happened to me recently, so I rang the person next day and said, "Are you OK? I sensed you were in some kind of danger." I felt such an idiot when they told me they were fine, but maybe that prayer had prevented a disaster? We have access to the greatest power in the universe – if only we would remember to use it more often!

"Ask for what you need… If your child asks for bread, do you trick him with sawdust? If he asks for fish, do you scare him with a live snake on his plate? As bad as you are, you wouldn't think of such a thing. You're at least decent to your own children. So don't you think the God who conceived you in love will be even better?"

Matthew 7:7–10 (MSG)

Lord, when my children were small I could protect and comfort them, but now when hard things happen to them I feel so worried when I can't make things better any more. Please change me from a worrier into a prayer warrior.

14
Losing Faith in Faith

A friend of mine has been going through a terrible family experience lately. She told me, "I feel as if I am only hanging in there by the threads of my faith."

"Suppose you asked Jesus to show you what those 'threads' look like," I suggested.

She obviously thought I was mad, but after closing her eyes she exclaimed, "Oh, the threads are made of gold!" A week later she emailed, "Things have got so much worse I can't hold on to those threads any longer. I feel my faith has snapped completely. So I've just had to let go and trust the Lord to hold me."

As I thought about that, I wondered if that "letting go" took even more faith than the "holding on". When we stop trusting in our faith and trust in the Lord alone, that's when He takes control! It must have taken so much faith for Peter to step out of the boat and walk on water towards Jesus. Yet it was when his faith left him and he began to sink that he was actually safest of all – because that is when Jesus caught hold of him.

You have to put up with every kind of aggravation...
Pure gold put in the fire comes out of it proved
pure; genuine faith put through this suffering
comes out proved genuine. When Jesus wraps
this all up, it's your faith, not your gold, that God
will have on display as evidence of his victory.

1 Peter 1:6–7 (MSG)

Lord, I can't see how the future is going to
work out, and the present is so difficult I don't
feel I can cope with it any longer. All I have for
certain is You! I'm very scared, but I know You
won't let go of me – ever!

15
Murmurations

I love watching the birds feeding on the table outside my window. Each species has its own personality: feisty robins; fat, lumbering pigeons; frenetically drumming woodpeckers; and gentle collared doves. However, I have to confess I loathe the spiteful starlings! They descend in a squealing flock, fighting each other as they greedily gobble up all the food, scaring all the other birds away. I was tut-tutting at them yesterday when a friend arrived who works with disturbed children.

"Some behave just like your starlings," she said, "but I always try to find something to love in each one – and then do my best to affirm it."

"Well, there's nothing to love or affirm about starlings!" I retorted. Then suddenly I remembered the bitterly cold winter afternoon when I first saw a murmuration. I stood open-mouthed, because it was the most beautiful thing I had ever seen. Literally millions of starlings were flying in the sunset, looping, swirling around the sky in perfect formation – for no other reason than the pure joy of living. For those glorious few minutes I suppose I can forgive starlings for everything!

It is so easy to dismiss people simply because they do or say things we don't like. Fortunately, Jesus sees the buried treasure in all of us, but like my friend and her "difficult children", He sometimes needs us to help Him dig that treasure out.

"But ask the… birds in the sky,
and they will tell you…
Which of all these does not know
that the hand of the Lord has done this?
In his hand is the life of every creature
and the breath of all mankind."

Job 12:7–10

Lord, it is You who causes starlings to dance
like that – I suppose because You enjoy
watching them too? Help me to see other
people from Your viewpoint.

16
Lobsters

I hate change! Even the kinds of changes I want involve unexpected losses that can feel painful and daunting. When a change I definitely *hadn't* planned hit me recently, it felt like a devastating earthquake, sweeping away people and surroundings I thought were permanent.

"What possible reason could You have, God, for letting this happen to me?" I demanded.

I believe He answered me one evening as I watched a TV documentary about lobsters. Apparently their soft little bodies could never survive in the sea without a tough outer shell to hold them together. While this "armour" protects them, it also traps them. They cannot grow larger unless, regularly throughout their seventy-year life span, they wriggle out of their shells and wait until their soft skin hardens into a new, larger one. Writhing out of their old shells, however, is so painful and exhausting that 15 per cent of lobsters die in the attempt, and many more are eaten by predators while they wait for their new shell to harden.

The TV presenter then showed us a lobster bigger than the six-foot fisherman who had just caught him, and explained,

"He's grown so big because he successfully changed his shell so many times." So if growth for a lobster depends on surviving change, then could God actually want to help me grow through this unpleasant upheaval? Perhaps it is during times of uncertainty and loss that faith grows faster and stronger?

After Job's "life-quaking" experience of grief and loss, he realized that his relationship with God had once been distant and academic, but through all he had suffered it had become an intimate friendship:

> *"I had only heard about you before,*
> *but now I have seen you with my own eyes."*
>
> Job 42:5 (NLT)

> *"Jesus, You are changing me, by Your Spirit*
> *You're making me like You."*
>
> Marilyn Baker (with permission)

17
A Persistent Mouse

Have you ever felt too disappointed to keep on and on praying for someone? The other morning I was feeling like that as I realized just how many years I've been praying for someone close to me, yet he only seems to keep drifting further away from God. Was it time to give up, I wondered.

Outside the window next to me my bird table stands on a tall, thin, iron pole, which I keep thickly coated with slippery Vaseline to discourage squirrels. Suddenly I noticed a very small mouse trying to climb the pole to get his breakfast. He would struggle up a few inches and then slither all the way back down. Over and over again he kept trying, each time managing to reach just a little bit higher up the pole. Finally, there he was! Right up on the table eating away happily – eyed suspiciously by a rather startled robin.

Beginning to wonder if God wanted to use the mouse to encourage me, I leafed through my Bible until I found Luke 11:5–9 where Jesus tells a story of a man who went to his neighbour, needing help, in the middle of the night. He had to go on and on banging on the door before his friend would

get up and give him what he needed. Jesus was making the point that prayer has to be persistent. I am sure we don't have to nag God into giving us what we want, but prayer is actually a spiritual battle, and the dark powers against us definitely do their best to intercept the prayers we launch heavenwards (Daniel 10:12–13).

> *"Ask and keep on asking, and it will be given to you."*
>
> Luke 11:9 (AMP)

> *Lord, I am so sorry I give up so quickly. Please make me as tenacious as that little mouse!*

18
Recycling on a Grand Scale

I had an email from Judy yesterday, telling me about the events that are rocking her life. Finally she added, "I'm trying to kick out the nasty question, 'Is Jesus powerful enough to get me through this?' But clinging to two words has really helped me! 'ALL THINGS.'"

Curious, I picked up my New Testament and was surprised how often these two words appear together: ALL THINGS were created through Jesus, He is before ALL THINGS, and in Him ALL THINGS hold together (Colossians 1:16–17). He knew that the Father had put ALL THINGS under His power (John 13:3), and He is able to bless us in ALL THINGS at all times (2 Corinthians 9:8). Best of all, He is able to bring good for us out of ALL THINGS – the good, the bad, and the ugly (Romans 8:28).

This morning Judy emailed again. "I was helping my daughter with her school project on water when I had a Eureka moment! I suddenly realized that God knew the only way He could provide a home for us on Earth was to give us water – but stagnant ponds wouldn't keep us alive. So He sends down fresh rain, then channels it in rivers, to the sea, where He has it sucked up again to purify, distil, and desalinate it in the clouds – ready to come back down again as rain. Someone who could think all that up will surely find a solution to my problems!"

"God is all-powerful...
No one can tell him what to do,
or say to him, 'You have done wrong.'
Instead, glorify his mighty works...
God is greater than we can understand...
He draws up the water vapor
and then distills it into rain.
The rain pours down from the clouds,
and everyone benefits."

Job 36:22, 26–28 (NLT)

My Lord and my God, You are awesome!

19
Another Side of God

"I always longed for the sort of mother who loved me," said Beth, "but my mum never could. I've always hoped she'd change – but she never has."

Through my work I meet a lot of people like Beth. Perhaps their mothers were ill, emotionally distant, or just too busy. Even as an adult Beth still feels an empty hole inside her where she longs to be mothered.

God wants to be our primary source of love and security because He knows how easily human love can fail us. However, that can be a problem when it's "mothering love" we crave because we tend to picture God as a father – and Jesus is obviously masculine. It was a great relief to me to discover that, in the Old Testament, the Holy Spirit is always referred to as feminine – the softer, gentler, cherishing side of God. He wants us to be able to relate to whichever side of Him we most need at the time. That might be the strong, protective, providing, affirming love of a father or, on other occasions, a God who cuddles and tenderly sings over us.

The Bible gives us several references to this "motherly" side of God, which are reassuringly different from the stern, punishing, uncaring picture we so often have of Him.

Like a baby content in its mother's arms,
my soul is a baby content.

Psalm 131:2 (MSG)

"As a mother comforts her child,
so will I comfort you;
and you will be comforted."

Isaiah 66:13

"Can a mother forget the baby at her breast
and have no compassion on the child she has
borne?
Though she may forget,
I will not forget you!"

Isaiah 49:15

Lord, I want to live, move and exist hidden
inside You, safe as an unborn baby (Acts 17:28).

20
Running the Race

My TV screen is full of the Olympic Games right now. I enjoy watching it all but hate seeing the contrast between the ecstatic faces of the medal winners and the tear-stained faces of competitors who didn't quite make the first three. They trained just as hard as the winners and made quite as many sacrifices – but they go away feeling disappointed failures.

What a relief that God's values are so totally different! Achievements are not His priority. He does not keep His gold medals for people who succeed in everything they do. It is faithfulness that God prizes. Hebrews 12:1–2 says, "Let us run with perseverance the race marked out for us, fixing our eyes on Jesus."

We all have our own personal racetrack. It might be leading an international ministry or a thriving church. Yet it is just as important in God's eyes if we are a full-time carer for a difficult person or a doing a dull job no one seems to appreciate. Doggedly keeping on right to the finish is what God rewards, and "fixing our eyes on Jesus" makes that possible.

Whatever our racetrack looks like, we might trip sometimes, or give up completely for a while, but with God, "failure isn't final". It simply gives Him the chance to demonstrate how good He is at getting us back on track again!

> *I press on to reach the end of the race and receive the heavenly prize for which God, through Christ Jesus, is calling us.*
>
> Philippians 3:14 (NLT)

Jesus, I know the "race" You had to run meant years of misunderstanding, rejection, hard work, and finally agony on the cross. My love, trust, and eternal life were the prize that kept You going, and Your never-ending company will be mine!

21
Taking Shelter

My Granny had an air-raid shelter in her garden. When I was four, the war had not long been over so it was still a clean, comfortable hideout under a mound of earth in her vegetable patch. I made it my "secret home", with rugs on the bed, crockery, and my graffiti all over the walls. I disappeared in there whenever Grandpa was cross or the kids next door shouted rude things over the fence. It felt safe.

I think the need for a place that we can call "home" runs very deep in us all: somewhere we feel we belong, where we are safe enough to kick off our shoes and be ourselves. Perhaps God created us with this longing because He wants to be our "hiding place" and for us to feel "at home" in Him?

I've never been very confident; shyness often makes me nervous of crowds or difficult situations. So I'm trying to remember, whenever I feel scared, to picture myself hiding in God – like I once escaped into my granny's dugout. Once I know I'm wrapped around by Him I find I can talk and act confidently because I no longer feel vulnerable. My "life is now hidden with Christ in God" (Colossians 3:3).

King David had many ways of seeing God: as a rock shelter, a high tower, a shield – even a mother hen. So perhaps it is all right for me to see Him like my granny's dugout? "But let them all be glad… who turn aside to hide themselves in you" (Psalm 5:11, TPT).

> *He who dwells in the secret place of the Most High*
> *Shall abide under the shadow of the Almighty.*
> *I will say of the Lord, "He is my refuge and my fortress… in Him I will trust."*
>
> Psalm 91:1–2 (NKJV)

Lord, I love the fact that I live in You, but You also live in me! So the moment I step into the supermarket – God Almighty enters the building!

22
A Wiggling Maggot

All summer God felt far away – our relationship seemed lifeless and boring. "What's wrong?" I prayed desperately one morning – and I believe He answered me through a wiggly maggot. Wondering if the apples on my tree were ripe yet, I bit into a large red one – and there he was, busily turning its core rotten. As I chucked the apple away I distinctly heard the word "resentment".

A situation has been making life extremely difficult for some time. Obviously I have prayed long and hard, but since nothing appeared to change, was I beginning to resent God for ignoring me?

Giving God positive emotions, like praise and adoration, feels right, but handing Him my anger seemed wrong! So could I have been hiding it, even from myself, like the maggot inside the apple? It began to dawn on me that really close relationships depend on emotional honesty, so surely God must want me to share *all* my feelings with Him – however unpleasant.

So I stood under my fruit tree and told God just how angry I was. When David says "cast your burden upon the Lord" in

Psalm 55:22 (NASB), he uses a very strong word which we could translate "hurl" or "fling away violently". I had sent both apple and maggot flying into the compost with that kind of disgusted energy! So obviously I needed to deal with my anger burden in the same decisive way!

When I was… bitter, totally consumed by envy…
I was… a dumb ox in your very presence.
I'm still in your presence,
but you've taken my hand.

Psalm 73:21–22 (MSG)

Lord, I'm sorry I hurt You by clinging on to my hurt and resentment. I realize it could have permanently damaged my relationship with You. Thank You for rescuing me.

23
Putting Down Then Picking Up

My difficult situation seemed to be growing worse until it hampered most areas of my life – and sinister questions began to pester me. Why, just when I was happy and had everything I most wanted in life, was God allowing all these painful losses? Perhaps He isn't as loving as I'd always thought?

One day, as I drove to church, I was feeling exhausted by all these doubts and conflicting thoughts. Not only were they rocking my faith, but they were also causing fear of the future and anger I could no longer control. Why wasn't I able, any more, to give all these negative feelings over to God and exchange them for His peace? There had to be a reason!

Suddenly I remembered something I had learnt during my counselling training. Anger and its companion – fear – are

often caused by blocked goals, by something we wanted and planned, but which is suddenly taken away from us. A lot of the goals I've been aiming at are disappearing, but surely they were God's desires too?

That evening our minister only seemed to be talking to me. "When we pray hard for ages trying to get God to change our circumstances, it could be that it is our *attitude* to those circumstances that needs changing. Jesus once said, 'If you want to be committed to Me, you'll need to be willing to put down your own plans and pick up Mine instead [Matthew 16:24]. So trust Me, My plans are always the best!'"

I did some serious "putting down and picking up" before I went home that evening.

> *"Anyone who intends to come with me has to let me lead. You're not in the driver's seat... What kind of a deal is it to get everything you want but lose yourself?"*
>
> Matthew 16:24–26 (MSG)

Thank You, Lord, that You always give the best to those who leave the choice to You.

24
The God of Tiny Details

My friend Sally loves photography, and she enjoys taking shots from unconventional angles. I sat for a long time gazing at the picture she sent me by email this morning before I recognized what it was! Then I gasped, "Lord, why did You bother to do all that, just for a weed?" Sally had taken a close up of a hawksbeard seed-head, showing the seeds fitting into an intricate pattern while their fluffy white parachutes waited above, ready to carry them away. All that beauty and designer skill, just for something I spray with weedkiller!

I know Sally is facing major family problems, so what she said in her email impacted me as much as her photo: "Surely the God who created such intricate detail cares deeply about my special daughter."

I think it must take far more faith to believe that the natural world just happened, rather than recognizing that everything was carefully designed by an intelligence infinitely greater than we could possibly fathom. Because all things were created in, for, and through Jesus (Colossians 1:16), it is no wonder He tells us not to worry!

"Consider how the wild flowers grow. They do not labour or spin. Yet I tell you, not even Solomon in all his splendour was dressed like one of these. If that is how God clothes the grass of the field, which is here today, and tomorrow is thrown into the fire, how much more will he clothe you – you of little faith!"

Luke 12:27–28

Lord Jesus, You not only created every tiny detail of this universe, but You also loved me beyond Your very life! How could I ever doubt Your ability to care for me?

"Were the whole realm of nature mine – that were a present far too small. Love so amazing so divine demands my life my soul my all."

Isaac Watts

25
Love Without Limits

Right now I'm relishing the discovery that God not only loves looking at minute details – like the patterns on a butterfly's wing – but He equally enjoys the vast expanses of space.

When David composed Psalm 103, people thought the universe ended with the last star their naked eyes could see. God, however, knew space is limitless, so when He wanted to tell us how much He loves us, He prompted David to write, "As high as the heavens are above the earth, so great is his love for those who fear [honour] him' (v11).

Most of us, when we try to imagine love as limitless as that, often feel, "Surely He can't love me when I sin so often?" He knew we would feel like that, so He gave David another illustration of

His remarkable ability to forgive: "As far as the east is from the west, so far has he removed our transgressions from us" (v12). People in those days also thought the earth was flat, so, in theory, you could walk from the east of it to the west – a long way but measurable. God wanted us to know that He removes our confessed sins an immeasurable and unreachable distance away! East and west are only a frame of reference for someone standing on Earth – invented by humans when they first drew maps. From God's viewpoint Earth is a ball, so there is no east or west, therefore the distance between them does not exist and cannot be measured.

> *But from everlasting to everlasting*
> *the Lord's love is with those who fear him,*
> *and his righteousness with their children's*
> *children.*
>
> Psalm 103:17

> *Lord, I can't find words to praise You*
> *adequately, but maybe it is the silent response*
> *of "all my inmost being" (Psalm 103:1) that*
> *You long for most?*

26
Doughnut Throwers

Yesterday morning Carol and I left at four in the morning to speak at a healing conference. As we neared our destination we stopped at a service station to change into our "best outfits" and to give our hair and faces some badly needed attention. As we sank onto a comfortable sofa to enjoy our coffee, I remember telling Carol how nice she looked in her new jacket. Suddenly, a young man at the counter began shouting, for no apparent reason, and then threw a large, squashy doughnut right into Carol's face, splattering her all over with sticky sugar and gooey jam.

After a long time in the Ladies with at least two packs of wet wipes we drove on – but Carol was very quiet. "I feel degraded," she admitted. "I know we've cleaned the mess so it won't show, but I still feel smeared and dirty. I can't possibly give a talk today." She was obviously shaken but suggested that we follow Jesus' instructions to "bless those who curse you, pray for those who ill-treat you" (Luke 6:28). As we drove, we prayed blessings over every area of that young man's life, and something began to happen: Carol's shoulders relaxed and she was giggling as she said, "Good job it wasn't a teapot!" That day she gave the most powerful talk I have ever heard!

Verbal "doughnut throwers" say things that sound sugar-sweet but are actually intended to make us feel inferior or in the wrong. These spiteful "doughnuts" can disturb our peace for days, but sending back blessings in return is a great way of avoiding their damage!

> *On her tongue is the law of kindness.*
>
> Proverbs 31:26 (NKJV)

Lord, help me to make it a rule to build people up by what I say and never to pull them down.

27
Message in the Snow

I'm always delighted when I see an email from Catherine in my inbox. When she describes her life in the wilds of Canada she makes me feel as though I'm there with her. After years of telling me about lakes and forests she began to let me into a deeper level of friendship:

"When I was small I didn't know about mental illness, so I couldn't understand why my Mom did such dreadful things to me when Dad was working away. I never told anyone; I just thought I must be wicked enough to deserve such terrible beatings.

"One night when I was six I wrote a letter to Jesus asking if I could belong to Him; then I put it into a polythene bag and threw it out of my bedroom window into the snow. I was sure He picked it up. After that I never forgot that I was His, and as soon as I left home I found myself a church.

"After a few years, memories about my mother's sadistic cruelty began to surface, and I really squirmed every time I heard sermons on forgiveness. Then one day I had the privilege of meeting Henri Nouwen. I explained how I had realized, through my medical training, how ill my mother must have been and that I wanted to love and forgive her – but it felt impossible. Gently he said, 'First you must appreciate how much she, and you, were loved by Jesus.' Focusing on the amazing compassion of our Lord made a profound difference. As I began to see Mom through His eyes I was able to love and forgive as He does."

"Whoever comes to me I will never drive away.'"

John 6:37

Thank You, Jesus, that Your grace was able to turn Catherine into one of the happiest people I know.

28
God's Hand

It was the last night of a Christian conference. As John made his final appeal, hundreds surged forward. I noticed him jump down from the platform to stand by one fragile-looking girl who was sobbing. "I'm afraid I won't keep all this up back home," I heard her say.

"Cop hold of my hand," John replied. "Don't let go. Promise?" Her little fingers could hardly reach round his huge fist so they soon came apart.

"This time, I'll be holding you," said John as his hand totally engulfed hers. "Twist and pull all you like, but you'll never get away from me."

When she finally gave up, he added, "Remember it will be God holding you, not you holding God!"

I remembered that the other day when I was out walking with my big son. I tripped violently over a tree root, but instantly his hand grabbed me and averted disaster.

Probably we all have moments when we worry that one day the Christian way of life may just prove too hard, or temptation will eventually knock us flat. I love the verse in Jude which assures us that God is "able to keep you from stumbling" (v24).

Maybe you wonder if your abilities and resources are actually enough to do the job you feel God is asking of you? Ezra might well have wondered that when he had to convey gold worth millions, and several thousand people, through 900 miles of bandit-infested desert from Babylon to Jerusalem. When they finished their apparently impossible journey, he calmly said, "The hand of our God was on us, and he protected us" (Ezra 8:31).

> "I have… covered you with the shadow of my hand –
> I who set the heavens in place,
> who laid the foundations of the earth."
>
> Isaiah 51:16

> Thank You, Father, that You say to me, "I am the Lord your God, who takes hold of your right hand" (Isaiah 41:13).

29
Choosing the Winner

I've been looking back through the last three months of my prayer journal, and realizing just how many times I've argued with God over the losses and problems which have been hitting me. Yet, lying alongside all my whinging, I can clearly see how He has been showing me more about His kindness, care, and compassion than I ever discovered during easier times. His "treasures of darkness", jewels we only mine in hard places (Isaiah 45:3, NKJV). I just wish I could stay permanently in that peaceful place of knowing He is carrying me, and has everything totally under His control. No sooner do I reach that glorious place of acceptance than I jump down again, screaming like a toddler in a tantrum.

Bereavement counsellors assure us that one day we reach "acceptance" – the point where we let go of life as it used to be and embrace something new. I'm discovering that acceptance – like forgiveness – doesn't just happen; you have to attempt it many times over. It's a fight, but a discovery I made in the bath one night is really helping me. I suddenly realized that the devil wants to use my painful situation to rob me of my relationship with the Lord, to ruin the work I do for Him, and to leave me lonely and bitter. The Lord, on the other hand, hopes to use *exactly the same* situation to show me how completely I can rely on Him and how tenderly He loves me. Two opposite game plans, but I am not a powerless football kicked between heaven and hell. I have the power to choose which side wins!

> *"Choose for yourselves this day whom you will serve."*
>
> Joshua 24:15

Lord, as You carry me into this new chapter, help me to take as many of Your "treasures" with me as I can possibly hold.

30
The Dragonfly Moment

When we were children, my brother and I lived by a muddy pond. The stagnant water smelt terrible but we loved watching the gloriously coloured dragonflies darting at high speed above the dark surface. One day we took a visitor to see them, and I was totally fascinated by what she told us: "For perhaps five long years, beautiful dragonflies are nothing but black bugs wiggling deep in the mud at the bottom of the pond. Then one day, for no reason anyone can discover, they begin trying to climb up a reed at the edge of the water. It's a huge struggle, and they must get a big fright as they eventually pop out of the water and see light for the first time ever! As their bodies begin to fill with oxygen, something amazing happens. Their black bug-skins split and out squirms a totally new creature. Once their four new gossamer wings have dried, they discover that they can fly free in the sunshine above the mud that once trapped them."

I've often wondered why God did not just create them as dragonflies in the first place. Perhaps He wanted to explain to us the difference between our limited lives down here on Earth

and the fantastic freedom we'll enjoy when we wake up one day in heaven?

> *Let me tell you something wonderful, a mystery I'll probably never fully understand. We're not all going to die – but we are all going to be changed... On signal from that trumpet from heaven, the dead will be up and out of their graves... never to die again. At the same moment and in the same way, we'll all be changed... mortal replaced by the immortal... Death swallowed by triumphant Life!*
>
> 1 Corinthians 15:51–54 (MSG)

Thank You, Lord, for giving us this "sure and certain hope" (Book of Common Prayer).

Acknowledgments

Unless otherwise stated Scripture quotations taken from the Holy Bible, New International Version Anglicised. Copyright © 1979, 1984, 2011 Biblica, formerly International Bible Society. Used by permission of Hodder & Stoughton Ltd, an Hachette UK company. All rights reserved. "NIV" is a registered trademark of Biblica. UK trademark number 1448790.

Scripture marked MSG are taken from The Message. Copyright © by Eugene H. Peterson 1993, 1994, 1995, 1996, 2000, 2001, 2002. Used by permission of NavPress Publishing Group.

Scripture quotations marked GNB are from the Good News Bible © 1994 published by the Bible Societies/HarperCollins Publishers Ltd UK, Good News Bible© American Bible Society 1966, 1971, 1976, 1992. Used with permission.

Scripture quotations marked KJV from The Authorized (King James) Version. Rights in the Authorized Version are vested in the Crown. Reproduced by permission of the Crown's patentee, Cambridge University Press.

Scripture quotations marked NKJV taken from the New King James Version. Copyright © 1982 by Thomas Nelson, Inc. Used by permission. All right reserved.

Scripture quotations marked AMP taken from the Amplified® Bible, Copyright © 1954, 1958, 1962, 1965, 1987 by The Lockman Foundation. Used by permission.

Scripture quotations marked TPT taken from The Passion Translation. Reprinted by permission of Broadstreet Publishing.

Scripture quotations marked NASB taken from the New American Standard Bible®, Copyright © 1960, 1962, 1963, 1968, 1971, 1972, 1973, 1975, 1977, 1995 by The Lockman Foundation. Used by permission.

Picture credits:
Alan Bedding: pp. 16–17, 36–37, 69, 89; Roger Chouler: header and footer, pp. 2–3, 6–7, 8–9, 22–23, 24–25, 29, 36–37, 52–53, 92–93; iStockPhoto.com: p. 19 © D4Fish, p. 21 © IvanJekic, p. 41 © Ron_Lane, p. 43 © jacktheflipper, p. 45 © xavierarnau, p. 49 © Reptile8488, p. 55 © shauni, p. 57 © sirichai_raksue, p. 61 © Mckyartstudio, p. 71 © M–image, p. 80–81 © Matko007, p. 82–83 © Eivaisia, p. 87 © VvoeVale, p. 91 © Mehmet Hilmi Barcin; Len Kerswill: pp. 13, 67, 75; Estelle Lobban: pp. 12, 14, 31, 32–33, 39, 42–43, 47, 58–59

Also available from Jennifer Rees Larcombe:

Jennifer Rees Larcombe blends observation and insight in these delightful uplifting reflections, celebrating the "God moments" that occur day by day. These 30 succinct meditations, beautifully illustrated, each with a prayer, will make a welcome companion and a gift to treasure.

978-0-85721-693-9

Here are reflections for days when the roof caves in and everything seems drab and cold. You want to pray, but the words won't come. Jennifer Rees Larcombe knows from experience how tough things can get, and brings together a collection of 40 meditations to bring light on dark days.

978-0-85721-694-6

www.lionhudson.com